MANCHESTER CITY

THE OFFICIAL ANNUAL 2021

g

A Grange Publication

© 2020. Published by Grange Communications Ltd., Edinburgh, under licence from Manchester City Football Club. Printed in the EU.

Edited & Written by David Clayton
Designed by Simon Thorley
Pictures © ManCity, Getty Images and PA Images
(thanks to Victoria Haydn/Tom Flathers/Matt McNulty)

ISBN 978-1-913034-99-3

CONTENTS

SEASON REVIEW
THE STORY OF CITY'S 2019/20 CAMPAIGN...

AUGUST

City started the season where they'd ended the previous campaign, by winning a trophy – the Community Shield in this instance – with a penalties win over Liverpool.

The Premier League campaign began with a thumping 5-0 win over West Ham United at the London Stadium. Then when Gabriel Jesus swept the ball home in added time against Spurs a week later, it looked like the perfect start – but a harsh VAR decision claimed

Aymeric Laporte had handled the ball as it came in and the goal was ruled out.

It was a cruel blow, especially as City had a goal ruled out against Spurs in the Champions League by VAR just a few months before.

A 3-1 win at Bournemouth was followed by a 4-0 home win over Brighton, meaning only VAR prevented a perfect August.

SEPTEMBER

City made a bad start to September, with a shock 3-2 defeat away to struggling Norwich. Knowing that the battle with Liverpool would again be intense, the Blues had already dropped five points out of a possible 15 and Liverpool had taken full advantage. If City were to win a third successive Premier League title, there could be no more slip-ups.

City returned to their ruthless best for the remaining league games in September, thrashing Watford 8-0 at the Etihad Stadium being – incredibly – 5-0 up after 18 minutes! Everton were then dispatched 3-1 at Goodison Park to leave the champions five points adrift of Liverpool with seven games played.

SEASON REVIEW
THE STORY OF CITY'S 2019/20 CAMPAIGN...

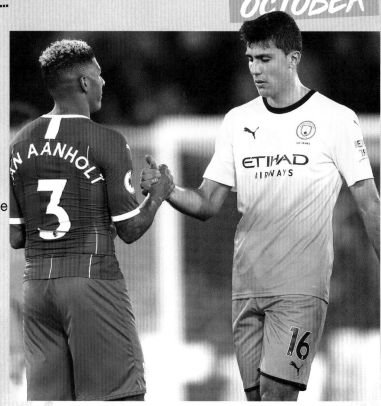

City's task became a mountain when Wolves performed a late smash and grab at the Etihad, with two late Adama Traore goals sealing a 2-0 win for the visitors. Already eight points behind a Liverpool side who had a 100% record, the champion's crown was slipping.

Of course, there was still plenty of time to catch the Merseysiders, but they would also need to drop points here and there – something that wasn't happening at that stage.

City bounced back with a 2-0 win at Crystal Palace and a 3-0 home win over Aston Villa, reducing the gap to Liverpool to six points going into November. There was still work to be done.

NOVEMBER

A narrow 2-1 victory over Southampton meant City travelled to Anfield knowing victory would put them just three points behind Jurgen Klopp's side – but with just one win away to Liverpool in 38 years, the omens weren't good. When a blatant handball in the Liverpool box was turned down by VAR, Liverpool broke to score at the other end and the day would only get worse, with City eventually losing 3-1.

The gap was now eight points instead of three and though a hard-fought 2-1 win over Chelsea brought some cheers, a late equaliser for Newcastle United at St James' Park meant two more points had been dropped and the champions ended the month 11 points adrift of a relentless Liverpool.

DECEMBER

A busy month began with a fine 4-1 win at Burnley, but a chastising 2-1 home defeat to an impressive Manchester United left City 14 points off the top.

Though Arsenal were comfortably beaten 3-0 at the Emirates and Leicester were beaten at the Etihad, City again uncharacteristically shot themselves in the foot just after Christmas where, despite having Ederson sent off, City led 2-0 away to Wolves – but the hosts recovered to win 3-2. For many people, it was hard to see how Liverpool could now ever be caught.

A 2-0 win over Sheffield United ended the year on a more positive note, but the fact that Liverpool just kept winning was hardly a cause for cheer.

JANUARY

City knew they had to put a run together if they were going to put any pressure on Liverpool. A 2-1 win over Everton followed by a 6-1 win away to Aston Villa proved the champions were not going to give up without a fight, but yet again, another shock result meant more points dropped.

City had trailed 1-0 to Crystal Palace before two late Sergio Aguero goals made it 2-1 – only for Fernandinho to score an own goal on full-time and make it 2-2. Now 13 points behind but having played two more games, the situation looked ever more difficult for Pep's men and only a bad run of form by Liverpool could change things.

City ended the month with a 1-0 win away to Sheffield United.

SEASON REVIEW
THE STORY OF CITY'S 2019/20 CAMPAIGN...

The general opinion was that one more slip-up and the 2019/20 title race was over, so a 2-0 defeat away to Tottenham meant Liverpool had an amazing 22-point lead at the top – even the most optimistic City fan accepted that was that!

Nonetheless City responded with wins over West Ham and Leicester City, and continued to progress in three other cup competitions (see elsewhere in the annual).

MARCH

After securing the Carabao Cup and reaching the FA Cup quarter-finals (not to mention beating Real Madrid away in the Champions League), City's immediate season ended in disappointment with a 2-0 defeat to Manchester United.

After that loss at Old Trafford, the Premier League was suspended as the COVID-19 pandemic hit global sport and there was even the question as to whether the season would be abandoned.

But after three months, football returned – just behind closed doors…

JUNE

City resumed their campaign with a 3-0 win over Arsenal and a 5-0 win over Burnley, making Liverpool wait a little while longer for their title confirmation, but an unfortunate 2-1 defeat to Chelsea meant City could no longer mathematically catch Klopp's men, who ended a 30-year wait to win the Premier League. It had been inevitable for some time, but the Blues ended the month with a 2-0 win at Newcastle to book a semi-final spot with Arsenal.

JULY

The goals continued to flow throughout July which had its ups and downs for City. A blistering start to the month came in the shape of thrashing Liverpool 4-0 at the Etihad. The newly-crowned Premier League champions were brought down to earth with a bump, as Kevin De Bruyne, Raheem Sterling and Phil Foden goals and an Alex Oxlade-Chamberlain own goal sealed the Merseysiders' biggest defeat of the campaign.

If a 1-0 loss to Southampton three days later was somewhat deflating, the 5-0 win over Newcastle United three days after that was anything but. Gabriel Jesus, Riyad Mahrez, a Fernandez own goal, Sterling and a sublime free-kick from David Silva were the scorers and the free-scoring Blues hit five again in the next match away to Brighton – Sterling bagged three and there were further strikes from Jesus and Bernardo.

It seemed the perfect form to go into the FA Cup semi-final with Arsenal, but a strangely subdued City would lose 2-0 at Wembley, with Pierre-Emerick Aubameyang bagging a goal in each half. A nervy 2-1 win over Bournemouth followed by a 4-0 win at Watford put the Blues back on track, and relegated Norwich were soundly beaten 5-0 at the Etihad in what was David Silva's final Premier League appearance for the Club.

That wrapped up the league campaign for City, who finished top scorers with 102 Premier League goals but still ended some 18 points adrift of champions Liverpool.

PLAYER OF THE YEAR:
KEVIN DE BRUYNE

The 2019/20 season was possibly Kevin De Bruyne's best ever – and that's saying something given his high levels of performance since joining City from Wolfsburg in 2015.

It led to 'KDB' being nominated for many awards, two of which he deservedly won. The City fans unanimously voted him as the Etihad Player of the Season – the third time he has won the honour in five years and with the stats he had by the end of it, it was no surprise.

De Bruyne played 48 games in all competitions and scored 16 goals, equalling his best ever tally, while assisting a further 23 – an outstanding contribution from a player who is quite rightly regarded as one of the world's very best attacking midfielders.

He seems to be reaching the very peak of his powers and will be the driving force in 2020/21 as City look to win back the Premier League title. Aged 29, he has already won eight major titles with the Blues and many believe he is destined to captain the side due to his inspirational style and natural leadership qualities.

It wasn't just the City supporters who recognised his efforts in 2019/20 – BBC Sport's pundits voted him their player of the season and in August 2020, he collected his first ever Premier League Player of the Season award to go alongside his second Premier League Playmaker of the Season honour for the 2019/20 campaign.

De Bruyne matched a competition record of 20 assists last season in the Premier League, equalling former Arsenal forward Thierry Henry's record for a single season set in 2002/03. KDB is the third Belgian in nine seasons to win the award after Vincent Kompany and Eden Hazard.

The Premier League award was decided by a public vote through the EA Sports website, votes from 20 Premier League club captains and a panel of football experts.

And though many felt Kevin should have been awarded the coveted PFA Player of the Year, the vote went to Liverpool skipper Jordan Henderson.

By the end of last season, De Bruyne had played 222 games for City, scored 57 goals, and made 89 assists for his team-mates. A wonderful footballer and well on the way to becoming one of the best players City have ever had.

Congratulations, Kevin!

GUESS WHO? #1

Can you figure out who the City players below are? We've disguised four images to hide the players' true identity – but can you use your detective skills to work out who they might be?

Answers on page 60&61

WORDSEARCH#1

See how many City players you can find in our Wordsearch – remember, the words could be horizontal, vertical or diagonal! There are 10 to find...

```
E  N  Y  U  R  B  E  D  O  L
D  N  W  R  L  K  J  D  F  R
E  Z  K  A  L  K  R  T  O  E
R  W  E  K  L  A  T  D  F  L
S  H  L  R  N  K  R  G  Y  Y
O  J  N  R  H  I  E  X  N  O
N  B  E  Y  G  A  N  R  E  D
D  B  M  O  X  B  M  M  D  X
G  N  I  L  R  E  T  S  O  N
X  A  G  U  E  R  O  K  F  K
```

AGUERO
BERNARDO
DEBRUYNE
DOYLE

EDERSON
FODEN
MAHREZ
RODRIGO

STERLING
WALKER

15

Answers on page 60&61

2020/21 SUMMER SIGNING:
NATHAN AKE

Dutch international Nathan Ake became City's second 2020 summer recruit after agreeing a five-year deal with the Club.

Ake's athleticism and experience – despite only being 25 – makes him a perfect addition to the City defence, where midfielder Fernandinho often had to cover during 2019/20 as injuries to Aymeric Laporte and John Stones took their toll.

Ake, who partners Liverpool's Virgil van Dijk for the Dutch national team, will look to move to the next level of his career after leaving relegated Bournemouth.

On signing, he said: "City have been the best side in England over the course of the last decade. Coming here is a dream for me. This is a top side full of world-class players. Everywhere you look in this squad there are big names with international pedigree.

"Pep is a manager admired across the world – what he's done in the game speaks for itself. The success he's had is unbelievable and the style of football he plays really appeals to me.

"I know I'm going to have to work hard to get into the side, but that's what I'm here to do. I'll do whatever I can to make an impact and help the team win silverware."

So, what can we expect from our new Dutch signing?

Technique, strength, and pace, plus he is a genuine threat from set-pieces. Bournemouth may have lost their top-flight status, but Ake is used to playing the ball out from the back and starting attacks from deep positions.

His journey began at VV Wilhelmus in Holland at the age of six, moving on to Den Haag two years later and then on to Eredivisie giants Feyenoord at the age of 12.

After impressing against Chelsea in a youth tournament, the then 16 year-old Ake joined Chelsea in 2011 and was an integral part of the Chelsea side that won the 2012 FA Youth Cup, later captaining the Chelsea Under-21s to the Premier League U21 title.

After progressing to the first team squad, Ake was then loaned out to gain further experience at Reading and then Watford before spending time with Bournemouth.

Though he then returned to Chelsea, Bournemouth made the move permanent in the summer of 2017, signing Ake for £20 million.

An ever-present in his first two seasons on the south coast, he would go on to play 121 times for the Cherries in total, scoring 11 goals.

He has won 13 senior caps for Holland.

NAME: Nathan Benjamin Ake
SQUAD NUMBER: To be confirmed
POSITION: Central defender
BORN: February 18, 1995
BIRTHPLACE: The Hague, Netherlands
SENIOR CLUBS PLAYED FOR: Chelsea, Reading (loan), Watford (loan), Bournemouth (loan), Bournemouth
CAREER APPEARANCES: 171 appearances, 12 goals

CROSSWORD

Can you solve the Manchester City crossword puzzle by working out the clues across and down?

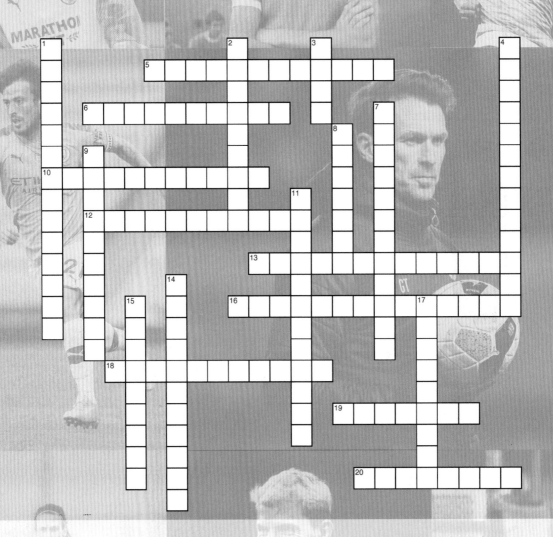

ACROSS

5 Our all-time record goal scorer. (6,6)
6 Spanish legend nicknamed 'El Mago'. (5,5)
10 Former Liverpool and Derby County keeper who joined City in 2019/20. (5,6)
12 City coach who joined Arsenal last season. (5,6)
13 City Women and England goalkeeper. (5,8)
16 City and France centre-back. (7,7)
18 City's Algerian winger. (5,6)
19 Team City thrashed in the 2019 FA Cup Final. (7)
20 One of our mascots. (8)

DOWN

1 City and England forward. (6,8)
2 City Women's new player-coach. (4,5)
3 Makers of City's 2020/21 kit. (4)
4 Belgian playmaker. (5,2,6)
7 City Women's new head coach. (6,6)
8 Our Brazilian goalkeeper. (7)
9 Teenage City player whose grandparents were both City legends. (5,5)
11 Brazilian City striker. (7,5)
14 Brazilian holding midfielder. (11)
15 Which former City legend has a stand named after him? (5,4)
17 The youngster nicknamed 'The Stockport Iniesta. (4,5)

Answers on page 60&61

SPOT THE BALL#1

Can you spot the ball? We've removed the real ball from the picture below, so you'll have to use detective work to try and figure out exactly which grid it's in – it's tricky and maybe not as obvious as it first looks – the players' faces may offer a few clues... or do they?

Answers on page 60&61

QUESTIONS

TOMMY DOYLE

One of City's brightest Academy graduates of the past few years is midfielder Tommy Doyle. A dynamic box-to-box player, he is a regular member of Pep Guardiola's first team squad and a young England player. Here, Tommy answers questions on everything from his favourite movie to advice for budding young stars of the future...

Full name: THOMAS GLYN DOYLE
Date of birth: 17-10-01
Place of birth: LEIGHTON CREWE
Squad number: 69
Junior clubs: SANDBACH EAGLES FC
Favourite food: CHICKEN PASTA
Favourite place to eat: MENAGERIE
Favourite drink: COKE
Netflix binge suggestion: MONEY HEIST
TV show you never miss: FAMILY GUY
Best book read: BLUE BLOOD – THE MIKE DOYLE STORY
Favourite movie: STEP BROTHERS
Favourite musician/band: CHRIS BROWN
Biggest influence on career: MY DAD
Favourite all-time player: STEVEN GERRARD
Other sports played: GOLF, TENNIS, SNOOKER, POOL, TABLE TENNIS

If you weren't a footballer what would you be? GOLFER
Who makes you laugh most? KARL PILKINGTON
Favourite holiday destination? MARBELLA
Best goal ever scored? v DERBY COUNTY FLOODLIT CUP FINAL
Best goal ever seen? TOO MANY!
Favourite stadium other than Etihad? CAMP NOU
Five people past or present you'd invite to dinner: MIKE DOYLE, GLYN PARDOE, RONALDO, ZINEDINE ZIDANE, STEVEN GERRARD
Favourite football boots: NIKE PHANTOM
Best piece of advice ever given to you? GO OUT AND PLAY
Advice you'd give anyone who wants to be a footballer: WORK HARDER THAN THE REST

FACTFILE
PHIL FODEN

BORN: 28/05/2000, Stockport, Cheshire
HEIGHT: 171cm
SQUAD NUMBER: 47
HOBBIES: Fishing

CAREER STATS:
DEBUT: 21 November 2017 v Feyenoord (UCL)
FIRST GOAL: 25 September 2018 v Oxford United (EFLC)
TOTAL GAMES: 63
TOTAL GOALS: 11
TOTAL ASSISTS: 10
YELLOW CARDS: 1
RED CARDS: 0
ENGLAND U21 CAPS: 15
GOALS: 4

HONOURS WON:
CITY (8)
PREMIER LEAGUE: 2017-18, 2018-19
FA CUP: 2018-19
EFL CUP: 2017-18, 2018-19, 2019-20
FA COMMUNITY SHIELD: 2018, 2019
FIFA U-17 WORLD CUP: 2017
UEFA EUROPEAN UNDER-17 CHAMPIONSHIP RUNNER-UP: 2017

INDIVIDUAL (4)
UEFA EUROPEAN UNDER-17 CHAMPIONSHIP TEAM OF THE TOURNAMENT: 2017
FIFA U-17 WORLD CUP GOLDEN BALL: 2017
BBC YOUNG SPORTS PERSONALITY OF THE YEAR: 2017
ALAN HARDAKER TROPHY: 2020

THE PERFECT MANCHESTER CITY PLAYER

Imagine you're a mad scientist and you can create a footballer using the best attributes of other players... what would your creation be capable of? Well, wonder no more! We've created the ultimate City player using the skills and various body parts of 12 existing players to create the perfect footballer...

HEAD: VINCENT KOMPANY

Our former captain was rarely beaten in the air and was a constant threat from set-pieces.

SHOULDERS: AYMERIC LAPORTE

Our Perfect Player will need broad shoulders for when he needs to defend – there are few better defenders than Aymeric so we'll use his shoulders.

HANDS: EDERSON

Though he is superb with the ball at his feet, Ederson can also throw a ball beyond the halfway line and makes excellent reflex saves – so Ederson's hands in case our Perfect Manchester City player ever needs to go in goal.

LEGS: KYLE WALKER

We need our Perfect Player to have plenty of pace and there's none quicker than Kyle Walker – so he will provide the legs.

RIGHT FOOT: BERNARDO SILVA

With the brilliant control and ability Bernardo possesses, his right foot will give our Perfect Player outrageous technical ability.

Our brilliant Spaniard – now sadly no longer part of the City squad – had intelligence and was sharp and clever. So, David's brain will control our Perfect Player.

Phil Foden is an imaginative player, always dreaming up new ways to pass, shoot and score goals – who better to have for imagination than one of Europe's most exciting talents?

EYES: KEVIN DE BRUYNE

The brilliant Belgian's vision has made him one of the best players on the planet – so we'll need his 360-degree vision.

NOSE: SERGIO AGUERO

Nobody sniffs out goals like our all-time record goal-scorer, so we'll take Sergio Aguero's nose for opportunities.

COURAGE: RAHEEM STERLING

Where does courage come from? It's a mixture of brain and heart and when it comes to standing tall and earning respect, there's few better than Raheem Sterling.

HEART: FERNANDINHO

Quiet and unassuming, Fernandinho also has a big heart and is one of our bravest players, going into challenges with no fear – so Ferna's heart for when the going gets tough.

LEFT FOOT: RIYAD MAHREZ

The Algerian's poise and balance are key to his style of play and he is often unrivalled with the ball at his favoured left-foot.

2020/21 SUMMER SIGNING:
FERRAN TORRES

Ferran Torres became City's first 2020 summer signing when he penned a five-year deal after joining from Valencia. Torres is a right winger by trade and during the 2019/20 campaign, he made 44 appearances for Valencia, scoring six goals.

"I am so happy to be joining City," Torres said. "Every player wants to be involved in attacking teams and Manchester City are one of the most attacking in world football.

"Pep encourages a really open, aggressive style, which I love, and he is a manager with a proven track record of improving players. To have him overseeing my development is a dream.

"City have won plenty of trophies in the last 10 years and I hope I can play a role in continuing that success."

A boyhood Valencia fan who had David Villa as his idol, Torres can also play on the left wing or play through the middle. An exciting prospect, he has pace and enjoys dribbling and taking defenders on, and is comfortable with both his left and right foot.

Born in a leap year – which means he officially only gets to celebrate his birthday every four years - Torres fits the bill of upcoming talent that Pep Guardiola wants to rebuild his team with.

He made his first-team debut for Valencia as a 17 year-old in November 2017 and went on to become the youngest player to make 50 La Liga appearances for the club, reaching that landmark on 23 November 2019 in a 2-1 defeat at Real Betis aged 19 years and 324 days – quite an achievement for a teenager.

In 2019, Torres won his first major trophy as Valencia won the Copa del Rey – the Spanish version of the FA Cup. In total, he made 97 appearances for Valencia's senior team, scoring nine goals and providing 12 assists.

He has been capped by Spain at U17, U19 and U21 level and tasted success, winning the European U17 Championships in 2017 and the European U19 Championships in 2019.

In the 2019 final, he scored both goals in a 2-0 win over Portugal alongside Eric Garcia – and was subsequently named Player of the Tournament for his performances throughout.

His acquisition is thought to be as a direct replacement for Leroy Sane who joined Bayern Munich during July 2020.

FACTFILE:
FERRAN TORRES

NAME: Ferran Torres Garcia
SQUAD NUMBER: To be confirmed
POSITION: Winger
BORN: February 29, 2000
BIRTHPLACE: Folos, Spain
SENIOR CLUBS PLAYED FOR: Valencia B, Valencia
CAREER APPEARANCES: 109 appearances, 10 goals

THE BIG CITY QUIZ 2020...

You might think you know a lot about City, but this quiz will test your knowledge to the maximum! There are some tough questions in the four sections here that you might need help with – but see how you go!

HISTORY SECTION:

1. Which year did the Club become Manchester City?
a) 1894 b) 1888 c) 1905

2. How many times have City won the top division title (First Division and Premier League)?
a) 4 b) 5 c) 6

3. How long was Maine Road City's home?
a) 50 years b) 80 years c) 90 years

4. Which home nation was legendary winger Billy Meredith from?
a) Wales b) Scotland c) England

5. Who did Sergio Aguero replace as the Club's record goal-scorer?
a) Niall Quinn b) Billy Meredith c) Eric Brook

6. Who scored City's first ever Champions League goal?
a) Sergio Aguero b) Aleksandar Kolarov
c) Edin Dzeko

7. Which club did Vincent Kompany join City from?
a) Anderlecht b) PSV Eindhoven c) Hamburg

8. True or false? Pep Guardiola once had a trial with City during his playing days?

9. After winning the League Cup in 1976, how many years would it be before City next won a trophy?
a) 30 years b) 35 years c) 40 years

10. Which team did City beat 10-1 in November 1987?
a) Leeds United b) Watford c) Huddersfield Town

2019/20 SECTION:

11. Which shirt number did Sergio Aguero have before he took the No.10 shirt?
a) 16 b) 21 c) 33

12. Who did City beat in the 2019 FA Community Shield?
a) Manchester United b) Arsenal c) Liverpool

13. Which country does Oleksandr Zinchenko represent?
a) Ukraine b) Russia c) Belarus

14. Who was City captain for the 2019/20 season?

15. Who did City beat in the 2019/20 Carabao Cup final?

16. Where was Raheem Sterling born?
a) England b) Jamaica c) Denmark

17. Who was the Manchester City Women coach that left for New York City FC?

18. Who was City's first 'behind closed doors' game against after the lockdown?
a) Burnley b) Leicester City c) Arsenal

19. How many years had David Silva played for City before he left the club?
a) 8 b) 10 c) 12

20. City beat Real Madrid 2-1 in the Bernabeu Champions League first leg – but who scored the goals?
a) Jesus and De Bruyne b) Sterling and Jesus
c) De Bruyne and Aguero

Answers on page 60-61

THE BIG CITY QUIZ 2020...

CONTINUED!

21. Which team does Kyle Walker support?
a) Sheffield Wednesday b) Sheffield United
c) Leeds United

22. Where were Phil Foden and Taylor Harwood Bellis both born?
a) Manchester b) Birmingham c) Stockport

23. Which former City boss is now manager of Italy?
a) Roberto Mancini b) Manuel Pellegrini
c) Sven-Goran Eriksson

24. At which time did Sergio Aguero score the winning goal against QPR in 2012?
a) 91:20 b) 93:20 c) 94:20

25. Which one of these companies has never made City's kit?
a) Nike b) PUMA c) Adidas

26. Which club did Kevin De Bruyne join City from?
a) Chelsea b) Werder Bremen c) Wolfsburg

27. Which City player has not played in the German Bundesliga?
a) Ilkay Gundogan b) Riyad Mahrez
c) Leroy Sane

28. Bernardo Silva joined City from which club?
a) Monaco b) Benfica c) Sporting Lisbon

29. What is the Etihad Stadium capacity?
a) 52,500 b) 54,750 c) 55,097

30. Which nickname have City NOT been given in the past few seasons?
a) The Incredibles b) The Fourmidables
c) The Centurions

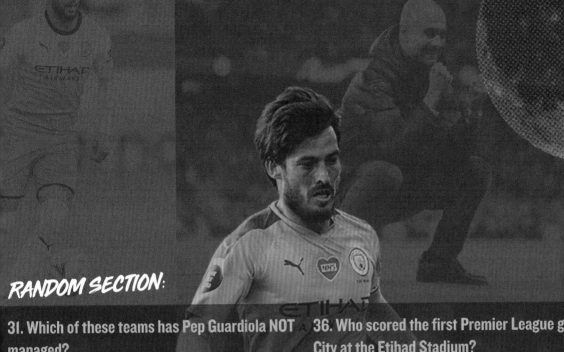

RANDOM SECTION:

31. Which of these teams has Pep Guardiola NOT managed?
a) Ajax b) Barcelona c) Bayern Munich

32. What is Sergio Aguero's nickname 'Kun' named after?
a) A cartoon character b) An Argentine actor
c) His grandfather

33. Which of these bands has NOT played a concert at the Etihad?
a) Queen b) Oasis c) Coldplay

34. Which is a famous City pie?
a) Chicken and gravy b) Cheese and carrot
c) Chicken Balti

35. Which of these companies has NOT been a City shirt sponsor?
a) Nissan b) Etihad c) Saab

36. Who scored the first Premier League goal for City at the Etihad Stadium?

37. Which club did Sergio Aguero join City from?
a) Independiente b) Real Madrid
c) Atletico Madrid

38. Between 2010 and 2020, how many managers have City had?
a) 2 b) 3 c) 4

39. What was the Amazon documentary on City called?
a) Everything is Something b) Unstoppable
c) All or Nothing

40. Which of these players has NOT captained City as of July 2020?
a) Ederson b) Kevin De Bruyne c) Sergio Aguero

Answers on page 60-61

SPOT THE BALL#2

Once again, we've removed the real ball from the picture below, so you'll have to use detective work to try and figure out exactly which grid it's in. It's tricky and maybe not as obvious as it first looks – the players' faces may offer a few clues... or do they?

1 **2** **3** **4**

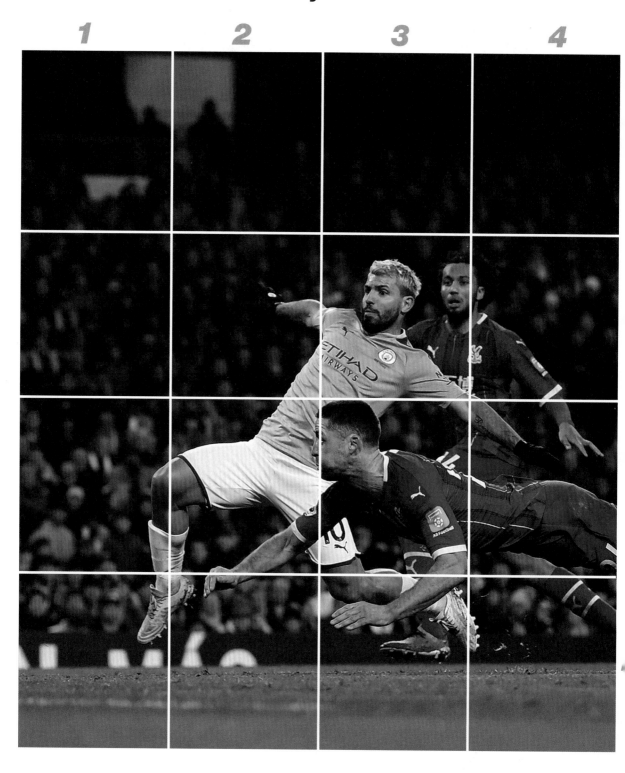

Answers on page 60&61

GUESS WHO?#2

Here are four more players we've disguised – can you work out who they are again...?

Answers on page 60&61

HOME SWEET HOME

When football restarted after the coronavirus pandemic, all matches had to be played behind closed doors. As you can see, our hardworking team made the Etihad look magnificent with various banners, flags and messaging. It's likely we will never see this sort of thing again, but it is a reminder of how everything changed in football and how City adjusted...

AMERICAN DREAMS

Meet two of City's new signings, both World Cup-winning USA internationals...

SAM MEWIS

Attacking midfielder Mewis, 27, is an all-action, never-say-die player with a winning mentality.

Going into the 2020/21 squad she had won 67 caps for her country and arrives from North Carolina Courage with whom she made 64 appearances, scoring 14 goals over a three-year period.

Of her move to City, Mewis said: "It's a little scary doing something new but I'm hoping that making this decision will continue to push me, develop me as a player and put me in the best position to make the Olympic squad.

"I wasn't actively seeking a move. My agent brought this to me over the summer and my ears perked up because it was Manchester City, an awesome club. And I'd heard so many good things about the team and the league."

FACTFILE:
SAM MEWIS

NAME: Samantha June Mewis
POSITION: Midfielder
SQUAD NUMBER: 22
DATE OF BIRTH: 09/10/1992
PREVIOUS CLUBS: Pali Blues, Boston Breakers Academy, Western New York Flash, North Carolina Courage

Welcome SAM MEWIS
2020/21 SIGNING
mancity.com

City have made some excellent signings this summer, but American duo Sam Mewis and Rose Lavelle have got supporters really excited.

Mewis and Lavelle were both part of the USA's FIFA World Cup winning squad and arrive with a reputation as two of the best midfielders in the world – and are arguably City's biggest signings yet.

ROSE LAVELLE

International team-mate and now Manchester City team-mate Rose Lavelle will further bolster the City midfield. The 25-year-old joins City from OL Reign and has so far won 45 caps for the USA.

Lavelle played six times for her country during the 2019 FIFA Women's World Cup, winning the bronze ball after scoring three goals. The Ohio-born star will wear the No.21 shirt this season. Lavelle admitted she and Mewis had discussed the move to City prior to signing deals with Gareth Taylor's side.

She said: "Me and Sam were definitely keeping each other in the loop with our decisions. I don't think it was the deciding factor for either of us, but it definitely helps to have a familiar face over there – not just a familiar face, but one of my best friends. To experience this with her is going to be awesome.

"I like to think that I'm a creative player, I hope I can bring some flair and playmaking into the final third. There's a lot of great attacking players I can hopefully combine with, but it's a very talented team so by no means am I going to walk in and play immediately – I have to earn that spot."

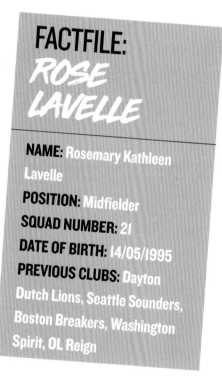

FACTFILE: ROSE LAVELLE

NAME: Rosemary Kathleen Lavelle

POSITION: Midfielder

SQUAD NUMBER: 21

DATE OF BIRTH: 14/05/1995

PREVIOUS CLUBS: Dayton Dutch Lions, Seattle Sounders, Boston Breakers, Washington Spirit, OL Reign

Welcome ROSE LAVELLE
2020/21 SIGNING
mancity.com

DESIGN YOUR OWN FOOTBALL BOOTS!

Imagine PUMA asked you to create a new football boot design – what would you do? Well, now you have the chance to show how creative you can be. It's your boot so let your imagination run wild and see what you come up with! Who knows, maybe these will be the boots you ask to be designed when you are playing for City!

COLOUR YOUR OWN FOOTBALL KIT!

Just like the football boots, PUMA have asked you to come up with a new design for City's away kit. What can you create? Will it be plain and simple, or something colourful and loud? It's your choice!

CARABAO KINGS!

More silverware for Pep's domestic cup kings...

City's domination of the Carabao Cup (also known as the League Cup) continued in 2019/20 with a third successive triumph.

Having won the competition in 2018 and 2019 with wins over Arsenal and Chelsea, City set about trying to make it a hat-trick of wins in succession, starting with a tricky-looking third round tie away to Preston North End.

Backed by more than 5,000 City fans, the game was over as a contest by half-time with goals from Raheem Sterling, Gabriel Jesus and a Ryan Ledson own goal giving Pep Guardiola's men a 3-0 lead – and with no further goals after the break, the cup holders cruised into Round 4.

Next up were Southampton at the Etihad and City again made light work of the opposition, with Nicolas Otamendi and two Sergio Aguero goals enough to complete a 3-1 win, gaining them a place in the quarter-finals.

For the second year in a row, City were drawn against League 1 side Oxford United and once again, the Blues headed home with a victory.

Joao Cancelo put City ahead before Matthew Taylor levelled for Oxford – but a Raheem Sterling double completed a 3-1 win and a place in the semi-finals.

The draw everyone wanted saw Manchester United drawn out the hat to face City over two legs. The first was at Old Trafford where a devastating attacking display by Pep's side saw City go in 3-0 up at the break thanks to goals from Bernardo, Mahrez and an Andreas Pereira own goal.

It could and should have been five, but City allowed a glimmer of hope to United and Marcus Rashford pulled one back after half-time meaning a 3-1 lead was taken into the

second leg at the Etihad. United would win that game 1-0, but City still progressed to the final having won 3-2 on aggregate.

Aston Villa were the surprise finalists at Wembley, where City started as strong favourites. Aguero and Rodrigo put City 2-0 up before Mbawna Samatta halved the deficit just before half-time. Villa improved after the break and only a superb Claudio Bravo save ensured City win the final 2-1.

It meant David Silva was able to lift his second trophy of the season as skipper, having already won the Community Shield against Liverpool the previous August.

With seven wins in total, only Liverpool – who have won the competition eight times – have a better record than City in the League Cup, who have now won it five times in seven years – 2014, 2016, 2018, 2019 and 2020.

WORDSEARCH#2

Find the words in the grid. Words can go horizontally, vertically and diagonally in all eight directions.

```
H  C  T  I  P  D  N  T  N  Q  G  D  C
M  B  J  C  N  D  L  X  P  E  K  D  H
L  N  G  K  W  F  R  B  M  E  S  G  Y
X  N  M  O  C  C  W  M  L  E  C  Z  M
T  M  R  M  V  N  A  K  L  R  O  V  H
S  C  W  R  C  R  V  N  A  E  R  V  L
D  E  T  H  G  N  P  X  B  F  E  Z  J
U  Z  V  O  I  L  Z  T  T  E  B  M  C
G  R  R  R  A  S  U  Z  O  R  O  N  X
O  P  N  Y  A  N  T  K  O  F  A  K  H
U  D  E  J  N  C  G  L  F  R  R  M  N
T  R  N  E  L  C  S  F  E  T  D  P  W
S  X  L  C  O  R  N  E  R  F  L  A  G
```

CORNERFLAG	**PROGRAMME**
CROWD	**REFEREE**
DUGOUT	**SCARVES**
FOOTBALL	**SCOREBOARD**
PITCH	**TUNNEL**
PLAYERS	**WHISTLE**

Answers on page 60&61

2020/21 SUMMER SIGNING:
PABLO MORENO

Pablo Moreno was the third signing to be announced by City in the summer transfer window.

The 18-year-old forward has penned a four-year deal and is very much 'one for the future'.

Moreno arrives from Juventus, where he has been part of the under-23 squad for the last two seasons. The teenage Spaniard is capable of playing anywhere across the front three or as an attacking midfielder and is considered to be an excellent prospect.

His career began at Barcelona's La Masia academy, where he broke several goalscoring records as he scored more than 200 goals across three age levels.

His reputation convinced Juventus to swoop for him in the summer of 2018 and he continued to develop in Italy. This season, he scored four goals in three UEFA Youth League games and in March 2019, he was named amongst the substitutes for a first team Serie A game against Genoa.

The teenager has won caps for Spain at under-18 level and last year he was part of the under-17 squad for the European Championships and World Cup. Moreno has chosen the No.38 shirt for the coming season.

FACTFILE:
PABLO MORENO TABOADA

NAME:
Pablo Moreno Taboada
POSITION:
Forward
SQUAD NUMBER:
38
DATE OF BIRTH:
03/05/2002
BORN:
Granada, Spain
PREVIOUS CLUBS:
Barcelona, Juventus

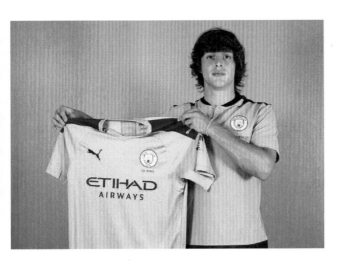

EXCITING SEASON AHEAD FOR MANCHESTER CITY WOMEN

Manchester City Women will begin an exciting new era in 2020/21 with new star players and a new head coach.

Gareth Taylor (pictured below) who was previously City's Under-18s coach takes over from Nick Cushing who left to work at New York City FC, and he will look to kick City on to the next level domestically and in Europe.

He will be assisted by Jill Scott, who will take on a player/coach role this season.

The global pandemic meant that the FA Women's Super League was finished early and the points-per-game calculation meant that despite City ending the shortened

season at the top of the table, the title instead was awarded to Chelsea.

City added two USA stars to their squad during the summer; World Cup winners Sam Mewis and Rose Lavelle will both add experience and competition for places.

Both play in midfield and, having won women's football's biggest prize, will be invaluable as City look to make an impression both at home and in the Champions League.

ROSE LAVELLE

They join a squad full of seasoned internationals that includes England captain Steph Houghton and Lionesses striker Ellen White.

Promising youngsters Lauren Hemp, Ellie Roebuck, Keira Walsh, Jess Park and Georgia Stanway will all look to continue to impress the new boss as well as the exciting talent of Canadian international Janine Beckie (pictured right).

Internationals Demi Stokes, Megan Campbell, Karen Bardsley and Caroline Weir – among other talented squad members – will give Taylor a chance of hitting the ground running in his first campaign as boss.

City have won six major domestic titles in six years – reclaiming the FAWSL title and achieving a long run in the Champions League are likely to be the main targets for Gareth Taylor's talented squad in 2020/21.

Get along and cheer the players on this season and be part of something special!

WORDSEARCH#3

Find the words in the grid. Words can go horizontally, vertically and diagonally in all eight directions.

```
P Q V B H C M V H Y N
Y S T Y R Y W E S G J
E T E V B A R E W K M
L A K I L J K J C I C
S N P S K O T U X Y S
D W H L T C B V V Y Y
R A Y S T E E T I H W
A Y R D O L C B W Z H
B Y T R C Q K J R F Q
P K G P S F T X Z T C
H O U G H T O N K Q Y
```

BARDSLEY
BECKIE
HOUGHTON
MEWIS
ROEBUCK

SCOTT
STANWAY
STOKES
WALSH
WHITE

RIYAD MAHREZ
FACTFILE

Total City stats

Premier League stats:
Appearances: 60
Goals: 18
Assists: 16

Champions League:
Appearances: 13
Goals: 2
Assists: 8

FA Cup stats:
Appearances: 10
Goals: 2
Assists: 1

League Cup:
Appearances: 10
Goals: 3
Assists: 3

FA Community Shield:
Appearances: 1
Goals: 0
Assists: 0

Total Appearances: 94
Total Goals: 25
Total Assists: 28

Yellow cards: 2
Red cards: 0

GABRIEL JESUS

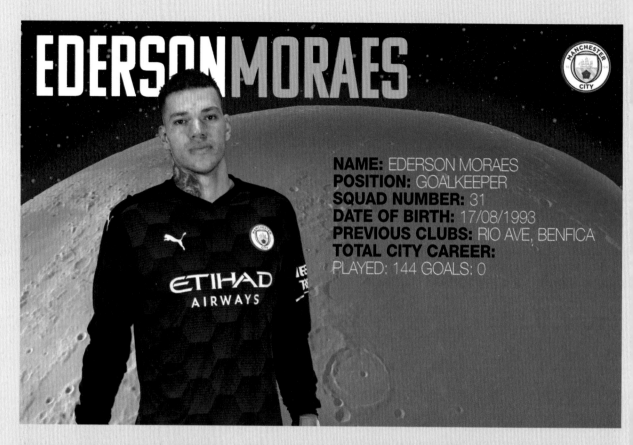

EDERSON MORAES

NAME: EDERSON MORAES
POSITION: GOALKEEPER
SQUAD NUMBER: 31
DATE OF BIRTH: 17/08/1993
PREVIOUS CLUBS: RIO AVE, BENFICA
TOTAL CITY CAREER:
PLAYED: 144 GOALS: 0

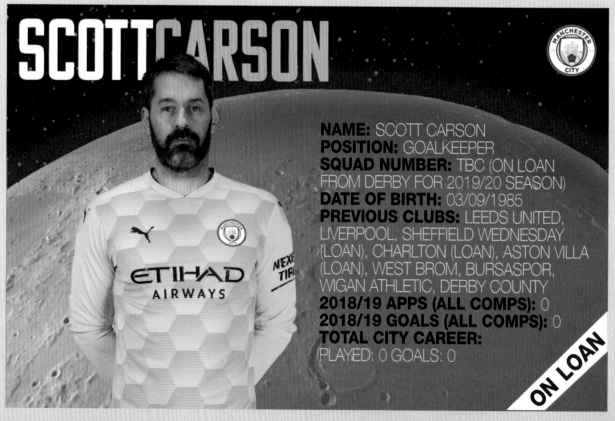

SCOTT CARSON

NAME: SCOTT CARSON
POSITION: GOALKEEPER
SQUAD NUMBER: TBC (ON LOAN FROM DERBY FOR 2019/20 SEASON)
DATE OF BIRTH: 03/09/1985
PREVIOUS CLUBS: LEEDS UNITED, LIVERPOOL, SHEFFIELD WEDNESDAY (LOAN), CHARLTON (LOAN), ASTON VILLA (LOAN), WEST BROM, BURSASPOR, WIGAN ATHLETIC, DERBY COUNTY
2018/19 APPS (ALL COMPS): 0
2018/19 GOALS (ALL COMPS): 0
TOTAL CITY CAREER:
PLAYED: 0 GOALS: 0

ON LOAN

BENJAMIN MENDY

NAME: BENJAMIN MENDY
POSITION: LEFT-BACK
SQUAD NUMBER: 22
DATE OF BIRTH: 17/07/1994
PREVIOUS CLUBS: LE HARVE, MARSEILLE, MONACO
TOTAL CITY CAREER:
PLAYED: 53 GOALS: 0

KYLE WALKER

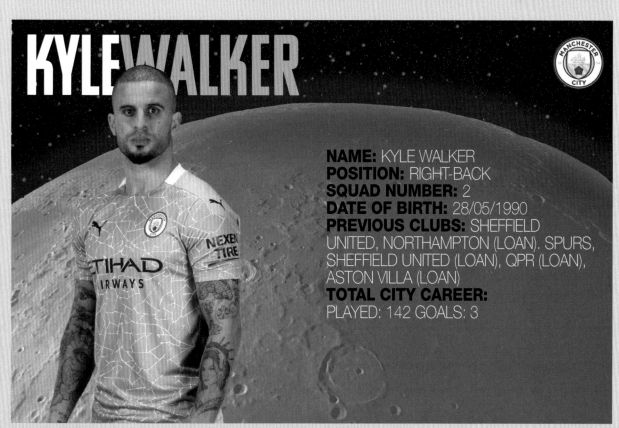

NAME: KYLE WALKER
POSITION: RIGHT-BACK
SQUAD NUMBER: 2
DATE OF BIRTH: 28/05/1990
PREVIOUS CLUBS: SHEFFIELD UNITED, NORTHAMPTON (LOAN), SPURS, SHEFFIELD UNITED (LOAN), QPR (LOAN), ASTON VILLA (LOAN)
TOTAL CITY CAREER:
PLAYED: 142 GOALS: 3

JOAOCANCELO

NAME: JOAO CANCELO
POSITION: RIGHT-BACK
SQUAD NUMBER: 27
DATE OF BIRTH: 27/05/1994
PREVIOUS CLUBS: BENFICA B,
BENFICA, VALENCIA, INTER MILAN,
JUVENTUS
TOTAL CITY CAREER:
PLAYED: 33 GOALS: 1

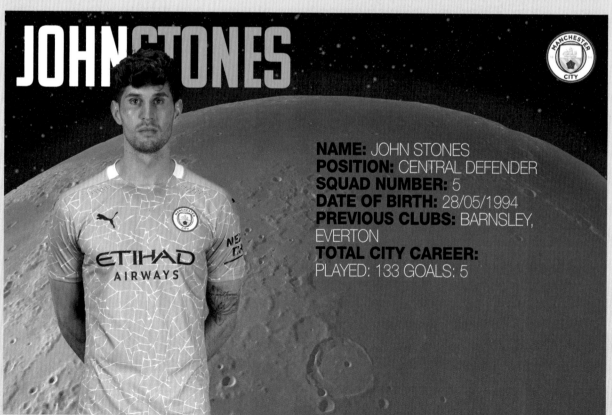

JOHNSTONES

NAME: JOHN STONES
POSITION: CENTRAL DEFENDER
SQUAD NUMBER: 5
DATE OF BIRTH: 28/05/1994
PREVIOUS CLUBS: BARNSLEY,
EVERTON
TOTAL CITY CAREER:
PLAYED: 133 GOALS: 5

NICOLAS OTAMENDI

NAME: NICOLAS OTAMENDI
POSITION: CENTRAL DEFENDER
SQUAD NUMBER: 30
DATE OF BIRTH: 12/02/1988
PREVIOUS CLUBS: VELEZ SARSFIELD, PORTO, VALENCIA, ATLETICO MINEIRO (LOAN)
TOTAL CITY CAREER:
PLAYED: 210 GOALS: 11

AYMERIC LAPORTE

NAME: AYMERIC LAPORTE
POSITION: CENTRAL DEFENDER
SQUAD NUMBER: 14
DATE OF BIRTH: 27/05/1994
PREVIOUS CLUBS: BASCONIA, BILBAO ATHLETIC, ATHLETIC BILBAO
TOTAL CITY CAREER:
PLAYED: 76 GOALS: 5

ERIC GARCIA

NAME: ERIC GARCIA
POSITION: DEFENDER
SQUAD NUMBER: 50
DATE OF BIRTH: 09/01/2001
PREVIOUS CLUBS: BARCELONA (YOUTH)
TOTAL CITY CAREER:
PLAYED: 15 GOALS: 0

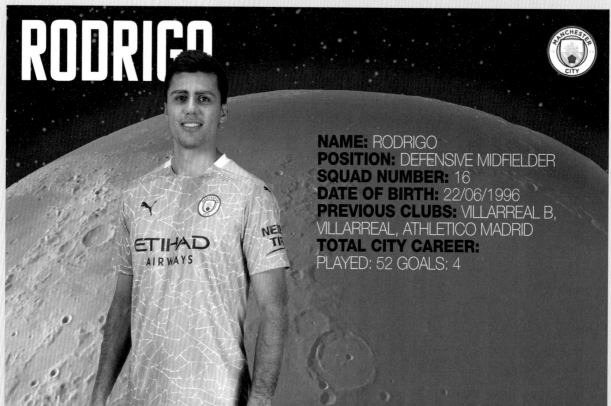

RODRIGO

NAME: RODRIGO
POSITION: DEFENSIVE MIDFIELDER
SQUAD NUMBER: 16
DATE OF BIRTH: 22/06/1996
PREVIOUS CLUBS: VILLARREAL B, VILLARREAL, ATHLETICO MADRID
TOTAL CITY CAREER:
PLAYED: 52 GOALS: 4

OLEKSANDRZINCHENKO

NAME: OLEKSANDR ZINCHENKO
POSITION: MIDFIELDER/FULL-BACK
SQUAD NUMBER: 11
DATE OF BIRTH: 15/12/1996
PREVIOUS CLUBS: UFA, PSV, JONG PSV
TOTAL CITY CAREER:
PLAYED: 68 GOALS: 2

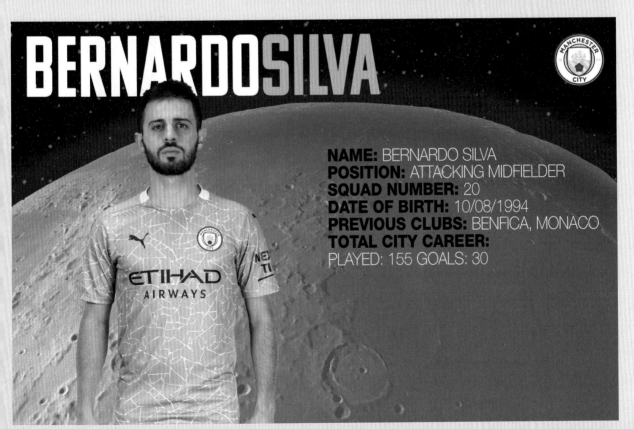

BERNARDOSILVA

NAME: BERNARDO SILVA
POSITION: ATTACKING MIDFIELDER
SQUAD NUMBER: 20
DATE OF BIRTH: 10/08/1994
PREVIOUS CLUBS: BENFICA, MONACO
TOTAL CITY CAREER:
PLAYED: 155 GOALS: 30

FERNANDINHO

NAME: FERNANDINHO
POSITION: MIDFIELDER
SQUAD NUMBER: 25
DATE OF BIRTH: 04/05/1985
PREVIOUS CLUBS: ATLÉTICO PARANAENSE, SHAKHTAR DONETSK
TOTAL CITY CAREER:
PLAYED: 314 GOALS: 23

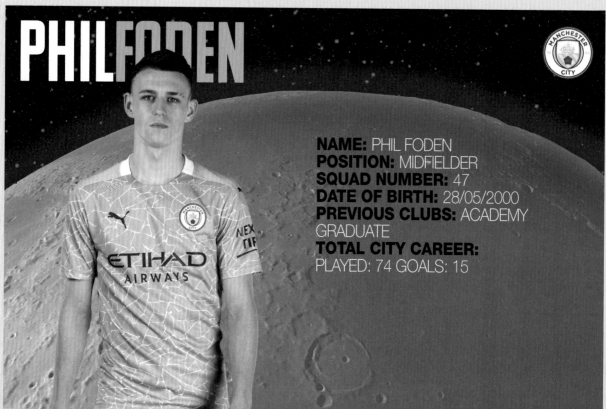

PHILFODEN

NAME: PHIL FODEN
POSITION: MIDFIELDER
SQUAD NUMBER: 47
DATE OF BIRTH: 28/05/2000
PREVIOUS CLUBS: ACADEMY GRADUATE
TOTAL CITY CAREER:
PLAYED: 74 GOALS: 15

ILKAY GUNDOGAN

NAME: ILKAY GUNDOGAN
POSITION: MIDFIELDER
SQUAD NUMBER: 8
DATE OF BIRTH: 24/10/1990
PREVIOUS CLUBS: VFL BOCHUM, FC NURNBERG, BORUSSIA DORTMUND
TOTAL CITY CAREER:
PLAYED: 164 GOALS: 22

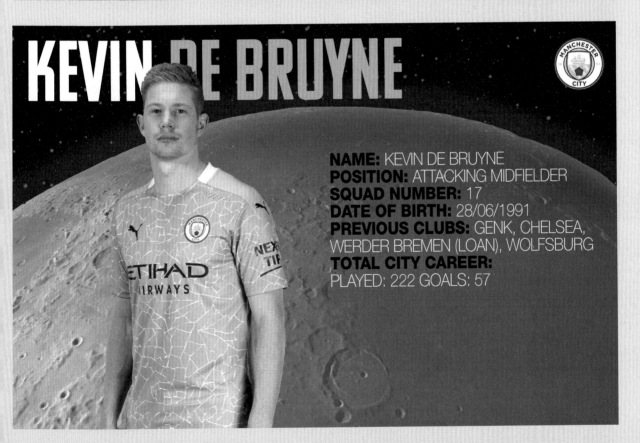

KEVIN DE BRUYNE

NAME: KEVIN DE BRUYNE
POSITION: ATTACKING MIDFIELDER
SQUAD NUMBER: 17
DATE OF BIRTH: 28/06/1991
PREVIOUS CLUBS: GENK, CHELSEA, WERDER BREMEN (LOAN), WOLFSBURG
TOTAL CITY CAREER:
PLAYED: 222 GOALS: 57

RAHEEMSTERLING

NAME: RAHEEM STERLING
POSITION: WINGER/FORWARD
SQUAD NUMBER: 7
DATE OF BIRTH: 08/12/1994
PREVIOUS CLUBS: QPR, LIVERPOOL
TOTAL CITY CAREER:
PLAYED: 243 GOALS: 100

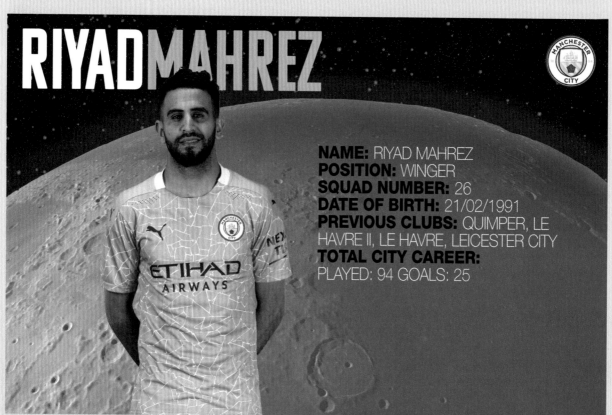

RIYADMAHREZ

NAME: RIYAD MAHREZ
POSITION: WINGER
SQUAD NUMBER: 26
DATE OF BIRTH: 21/02/1991
PREVIOUS CLUBS: QUIMPER, LE HAVRE II, LE HAVRE, LEICESTER CITY
TOTAL CITY CAREER:
PLAYED: 94 GOALS: 25

SERGIO AGUERO

NAME: SERGIO AGÜERO
POSITION: STRIKER
SQUAD NUMBER: 10
DATE OF BIRTH: 02/06/1988
PREVIOUS CLUBS: INDEPENDIENTE, ATLÉTICO MADRID
TOTAL CITY CAREER:
PLAYED: 370 GOALS: 254

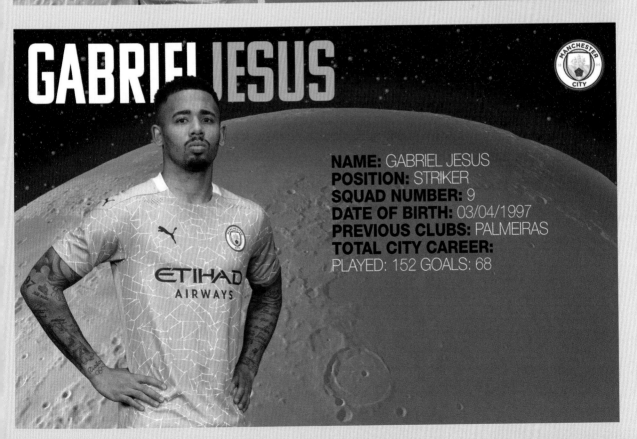

GABRIEL JESUS

NAME: GABRIEL JESUS
POSITION: STRIKER
SQUAD NUMBER: 9
DATE OF BIRTH: 03/04/1997
PREVIOUS CLUBS: PALMEIRAS
TOTAL CITY CAREER:
PLAYED: 152 GOALS: 68

MANCITY SQUADPROFILES 2020/21

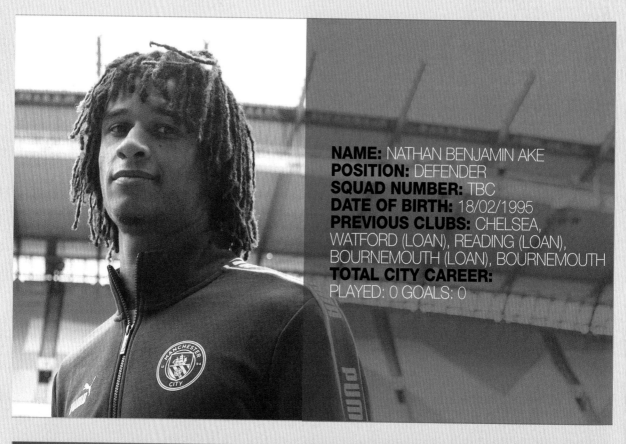

NAME: NATHAN BENJAMIN AKE
POSITION: DEFENDER
SQUAD NUMBER: TBC
DATE OF BIRTH: 18/02/1995
PREVIOUS CLUBS: CHELSEA,
WATFORD (LOAN), READING (LOAN),
BOURNEMOUTH (LOAN), BOURNEMOUTH
TOTAL CITY CAREER:
PLAYED: 0 GOALS: 0

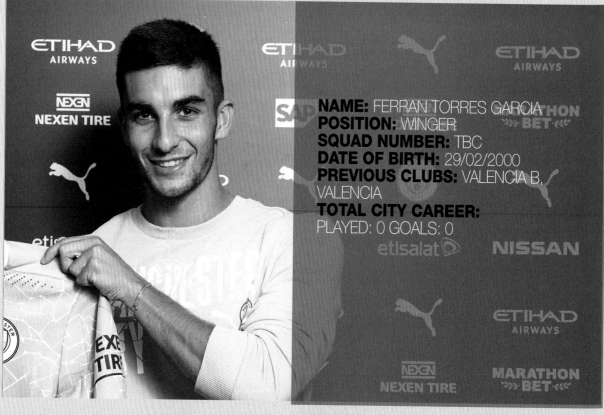

NAME: FERRAN TORRES GARCIA
POSITION: WINGER
SQUAD NUMBER: TBC
DATE OF BIRTH: 29/02/2000
PREVIOUS CLUBS: VALENCIA B,
VALENCIA
TOTAL CITY CAREER:
PLAYED: 0 GOALS: 0

SERGIO AGUERO

QUIZ AND PUZZLE ANSWERS

GUESS WHO? #1
(From page 14)

01 RODRIGO

02 KEVIN DE BRUYNE

03 BENJAMIN MENDY

04 SERGIO AGUERO

WORDSEARCH #1
(From page 15)

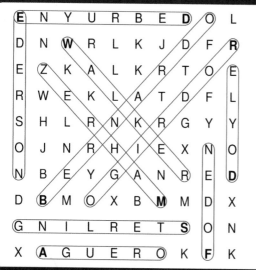

E	N	Y	U	R	B	E	D	O	L
D	N	W	R	L	K	J	D	F	R
E	Z	K	A	L	K	R	T	O	E
R	W	E	K	L	A	T	D	F	L
S	H	L	R	N	K	R	G	Y	Y
O	J	N	R	H	I	E	X	N	O
N	B	E	Y	G	A	N	R	E	D
D	B	M	O	X	B	M	M	D	X
G	N	I	L	R	E	T	S	O	N
X	A	G	U	E	R	O	K	F	K

CROSSWORD
(From page 18)

RAHEEMSTERLING
SERGIOAGUERO
JLISCOTT
PUMA
KEVINDEBRUYNE
DAVIDSILVA
GARETH
SCOTTCARSON
TOMMYDOYLE
MIKELARTETA
KARENBARDSLEY
COLINBELL
FERNANDINHO
AYMERICLAPORTE
TAYLOR
RIYADMAHREZ
HILFODE
WATFORD
MOONBEAM

SPOT THE BALL #1   6H
(From page 19)

	1	2	3	4	5	6	7	8
A								
B								
C								
D								
E								
F								
G								
H								

SPOT THE BALL #2   1B
(From page 30)

	1	2	3	4
A				
B				
C				
D				

GUESS WHO? #2 (From page 31)

01 BENJAMIN MENDY

02 BERNARDO SILVA

03 FERNANDINHO

04 NICOLAS OTAMENDI

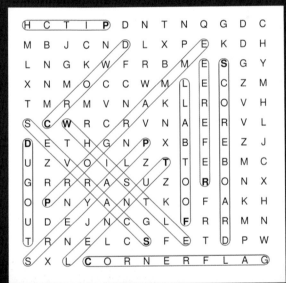

WORDSEARCH #2 (From page 40)

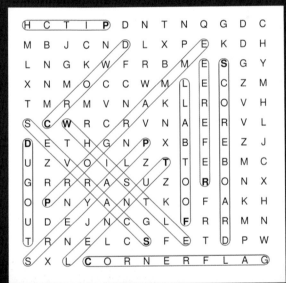

WORDSEARCH #3 (From page 45)

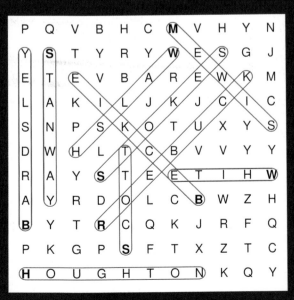

THE *BIG* CITY QUIZ 2021 (From page 26-29)

1) 1894
2) 6
3) 80 YEARS
4) WALES
5) ERIC BROOK
6) ALEKSANDAR KOLAROV
7) HAMBURG
8) TRUE
9) 35 YEARS
10) HUDDERSFIELD TOWN
11) 16
12) LIVERPOOL
13) UKRAINE
14) DAVID SILVA
15) ASTON VILLA
16) JAMAICA
17) NICK CUSHING
18) ARSENAL
19) 10
20) JESUS AND DE BRUYNE
21) SHEFFIELD UNITED
22) STOCKPORT
23) ROBERTO MANCINI
24) 94:20
25) ADIDAS
26) WOLFSBURG
27) RIYAD MAHREZ
28) MONACO
29) 55,097
30) THE INCREDIBLES
31) AJAX
32) A CARTOON CHARACTER
33) QUEEN
34) CHICKEN BALTI
35) NISSAN
36) DAVID SOMMEIL
37) ATLETICO MADRID
38) 3
39) ALL OR NOTHING
40) EDERSON

WHERE'S SERGIO?

Take a good look at this picture of thousands of City fans. Now take a closer look, because we've placed Sergio Aguero somewhere in the crowd! Get your magnifying glass out and see if you can find him…